Presented To

_____

From

_____

Date

_____

Promises & Blessings From God's Heart to Yours: A 365 Devotional Journal

Copyright © 2018 by DaySpring

First Edition, January 2019

Published by:

P.O. Box 1010
Siloam Springs, AR 72761
dayspring.com

Unless otherwise noted, all Scripture quotations are taken from the Christian Standard Bible®, Copyright © 2017 by Holman Bible Publishers. Used by permission. Christian Standard Bible® and CSB are federally registered trademarks of Holman Bible Publishers.

Printed in China

Designed by Jessica Wei

Prime: 91629

ISBN: 978-1-68408-681-8

PROMISES
— & —
BLESSINGS
From God's Heart to Yours

A 365 DEVOTIONAL JOURNAL

JANUARY 1

*W*e can look forward to the year ahead
with an unwavering confidence in God—
He loves us more than we can imagine,
wants us to live out the dreams He put in our hearts,
and cheers us on to fulfill His purpose for us.

*May He give you what your heart desires
and fulfill your whole purpose.*
PSALM 20:4

*O*ur walk with God can be closer
than we realize is possible.
With our spirit in tune with His will,
if the path in front of us is washed out
by the rains of life we will not lose our footing,
our courage, or our way.

I lift my eyes toward the mountains.
Where will my help come from? My help comes from the LORD,
the Maker of heaven and earth. He will not allow your foot to slip;
your Protector will not slumber.
PSALM 121:1-3

*G*ratitude confounds the enemy
and ignites the powers of heaven.
There are so many blessings and gifts
in our lives that we can be aware of and thankful for!

*And let the peace of Christ,
to which you were also called in one body, rule your hearts.
And be thankful.*
COLOSSIANS 3:15

One of the greatest blessings we can know
on a daily basis is God's amazing presence.
Having Him near changes everything.

*Your word is a lamp for my feet
and a light on my path.*
PSALM 119:105

There is so much God can do
in our lives that only He can—
strengthen us with His love,
fill us with His assurance,
bless us with His peace,
and hold us in His arms as we trust Him
with every detail of our day.

I pray that you, being rooted and firmly established in love,
may be able to comprehend with all the saints
what is the length and width, height and depth of God's love.
EPHESIANS 3:17-18

*H*ope is the gentle 'lift'
God puts beneath our dreams
while He prepares our hearts to see them come true—
may we never lose sight of the desires
He's placed within us.

Hope delayed makes the heart sick,
but desire fulfilled is a tree of life.
PROVERBS 13:12

*W*ith His fingers He suspends the universe,
and in His palm He holds each one of us.

Truly I tell you, if two of you on earth agree
about any matter that you pray for,
it will be done for you by My Father in heaven.
For where two or three are gathered together in My name,
I am there among them.
MATTHEW 18:19-20

The blessings of God are upon us—
blessings of love and blessings of kindness;
blessings of joy and blessings of laughter;
blessings of peace and
blessings of good things to come.

May the LORD bless you and protect you;
may the LORD make His face shine on you and
be gracious to you; may the LORD look with favor
on you and give you peace.
NUMBERS 6:24-26

Everywhere we go,
God calls us to be carriers of His love
and shiners of His light.

May the LORD's blessing be on you.
PSALM 129:8

God delivers 'just because' messages
from Him throughout our days:
a timely word, a kindness, a warm smile,
a favor, or anything that brings
a little joy into our lives.

The LORD your God will bless you...
and you will have abundant joy.
DEUTERONOMY 16:15

We can always rest in the welcoming,
loving arms of our Father when we call to Him,
experiencing His quick and confident voice as we pray.

Even before they call, I will answer;
while they are still speaking, I will hear.
ISAIAH 65:24

There are no limits to God's love for us,
what He desires to give us,
or what He can accomplish through us.
He delights in filling our lives
with unimaginable goodness—
it's the sweet reward of trusting Him.

Now to Him who is able to do above and beyond
all that we ask or think according to the power that works in us—
to Him be glory in the church and in Christ Jesus
to all generations, forever and ever.
EPHESIANS 3:20-21

JANUARY 13

*E*very day is a chance for God
to bless the work of our hands.
We are kind expressions of His love,
true examples of His mercy,
and genuine messengers of His joy.
When we let Him work through us,
there is a light emanating from our spirits
that brings warmth to others and glory to God.

Now may the God of peace Himself sanctify you completely.
I THESSALONIANS 5:23

*E*ach day, we can walk around
completely covered in His presence.
We can constantly know that protection, comfort,
and guidance wherever we go.

But let all who take refuge in You rejoice;
let them shout for joy forever.
May You shelter them,
and may those who love Your name boast about You.
PSALM 5:11

God does so much to get us where we are each day.
He works in ways that we have no idea about.
Every day we can walk in thankfulness
that His kingdom comes in us, His will is done in us,
right here, right now on earth as it is in heaven.

*For it is God who is working in you both to will
and to work according to His good purpose.*
PHILIPPIANS 2:13

With God, we can walk in peace,
allowing Him to lead us.
We can serve with humility,
allowing Him to teach us.
And we can hope with confidence,
allowing God to bless us.

Send Your light and Your truth; let them lead me.
PSALM 43:3

His is hope is a beacon—
a guide which constantly reminds us
that nothing is out of the scope of His ability.

*Now may the God of hope fill you with all joy
and peace as you believe,
so that you may overflow with hope
by the power of the Holy Spirit.*
ROMANS 15:13

There is so much to be thankful for,
in gray days, busy days, and even days
when everything seems to go wrong!
When it's gloomy, we depend on God
to brighten our lives with joy;
when we get too busy,
we trust in God to give us strength;
when things go wrong,
we lean on His grace to sustain us.

Give thanks to the LORD, for He is good;
His faithful love endures forever.
I CHRONICLES 16:34

JANUARY 19

*S*urrendering everything we have,
and everything we are, sounds scary.
But it's the only way to deep and lasting peace.

Know the God of your father,
and serve Him wholeheartedly and with a willing mind....
If you seek Him, He will be found by you.
I CHRONICLES 28:9

*J*oy is powerful and each person
is a transformer in His name!
The Lord lifts us up to strengthen those around us,
fill us with His peace, and bring us
the incredible riches of His kingdom.

The eyes of the LORD roam throughout the earth
to show Himself strong for those
who are wholeheartedly devoted to Him.
II CHRONICLES 16:9

*E*very day the Lord reminds us that He is for us,
and nothing outside His will can prevail against us.
He prays for us, and we are covered
by forgiveness and grace;
He loves us, and we are thought of constantly;
He values us, and each of us
is fulfilling a divine purpose.

You who seek God, take heart!
PSALM 69:32

No one guides better than the Holy Spirit.
It is possible to experience His gentle leadership
in all that we do.

Teach me to do Your will,
for You are my God.
May Your gracious Spirit lead me on level ground.
PSALM 143:10

*E*veryone who follows Christ can live in joy,
knowing we are serving with His hands and feet.
We can feel the warmth of His smile through us,
the touch of His hand through us,
and the love of His heart through us in all we do.

Serve the LORD with gladness;
come before Him with joyful songs.
PSALM 100:2

The Lord blesses His people
with the riches of His grace;
with the treasures of His love;
with the comfort of His mercies;
with the strength of His presence;
with the touch of His care.

If God is for us, who is against us?
He did not even spare His own Son,
but offered Him up for us all.
How will He not also with Him grant us everything?
ROMANS 8:31, 32

The Lord fills us with His strength each day.
He guides us along His path.
He shows us where we might effectively serve
and love those of His children.

*I pray that He may grant you,
according to the riches of His glory,
to be strengthened with power
in your inner being through His Spirit.*
EPHESIANS 3:16

There is no greater peace
than to walk in faith and obedience.

Fear God and keep His commands,
because this is for all humanity.
ECCLESIASTES 12:13

JANUARY 27

The Lord's mercy is available
to make us feel like a new person each day,
ready to face everything that comes our way
with a heavenly perspective.

May your whole spirit, soul, and body
be kept sound and blameless
at the coming of our Lord Jesus Christ.
I THESSALONIANS 5:23

Even in the midst of difficulties,
we can know His mighty power.
Even when we have made mistakes,
we can experience His tender mercy and forgiveness.
Even when someone has wronged us,
we can feel His grace sustaining and lifting us up.

*Let us fall into the LORD's hands
because His mercies are great.*
II SAMUEL 24:14

*L*aughter is a sound the Lord loves to hear.
His joy is our strength—
and the decision to walk in that joy today
will cast a beautiful light
on God's goodness.

Let us be self-controlled and put on the armor of faith and love,
and a helmet of the hope of salvation.
I THESSALONIANS 5:8

Forgiveness always leads to freedom,
because forgiveness is
one of the most powerful tools of peace.

If we confess our sins,
He is faithful and righteous to forgive us our sins
and to cleanse us from all unrighteousness.
I JOHN 1:9

God's works are wonderful—
we know that full well!
He shows us every detail
of His precious love when we ask.
Not just the things we can see,
but the things we will easily miss
without His guidance.

For You have made me rejoice, LORD,
by what You have done;
I will shout for joy because of the works of Your hands.
PSALM 92:4

Every day is filled with opportunities to love others,
in ways that genuinely translate
God's care for them even in the smallest ways.

The joy of the LORD is your strength.
NEHEMIAH 8:10

*W*hen we stay in tune with God,
He guides us toward those
who need His tender presence,
and He uses our hands to touch
the hearts of those who most need it.

May the Lord cause you to increase and overflow with love
for one another and for everyone.
I THESSALONIANS 3:12

The love of God for us is so great
that nothing can interrupt it, defuse it,
detain it, distract it, deplete it, cancel it,
overthrow it, or separate us from it.

As the Father has loved me,
I have also loved you.
Remain in My love.
JOHN 15:9

*E*ach of us has been blessed
by God with the capacity for a grateful heart,
which is the source of humility;
a joyful spirit, which is the well of strength;
and a peaceful soul, which is the reflection of trust.

I pray that your participation in the faith
may become effective through knowing every good thing
that is in us for the glory of Christ.
PHILEMON 1:6

The Lord can show us how to pray without anxiety
and receive His answers with all grace.
He can fill our lives with the peace
that passes understanding.

May the Lord of peace Himself
give you peace always in every way.
II THESSALONIANS 3:16

*A*s much as a person could possibly
have her thoughts toward God all day long,
it wouldn't match His thoughts about us,
which are on us constantly.

*I pray that you are prospering in every way
and are in good health,
just as your whole life is going well.*
III JOHN 1:2

*E*ach of us is hand-picked by God,
cultivated, created, and fashioned
into a marvelous light for this world.

God, who from my mother's womb set me apart
and called me by His grace,
was pleased to reveal His Son in me,
so that I could preach Him among the Gentiles.
GALATIANS 1:15, 16

*G*od can open our eyes
to every instance of His unique,
special, thoughtful diligence in our lives.
We can know the height, depth, and breadth
of His love for us and be able to pour
that love out to those around us.

God, how precious Your thoughts are to me;
how vast their sum is! If I counted them,
they would outnumber the grains of sand.
PSALM 139:17, 18

The Lord who loves us and holds us
in the palm of His hand wants to bless us each day—
in amazing, humbling, and breathtaking ways.

For as heaven is higher than earth,
so My ways are higher than your ways,
and My thoughts than your thoughts.
ISAIAH 55:9

*W*e are the rejoicing of God's heart.
It is great joy to feel His presence
as we go about our daily tasks,
tend to the smallest details of our to-do lists,
and share His love with those
He brings across our paths.

*I pray that the eyes of your heart may be enlightened
so that you may know what is the hope of His calling,
what is the wealth of His glorious inheritance in the saints.*
EPHESIANS 1:18

It's important for us to be patient
as the Lord continues to do His work in us—
what we are seeing now are His brush strokes,
not the final painting.

Jesus told him, "I am the way, the truth, and the life.
No one comes to the Father except through Me."
JOHN 14:6

God is a giver, and we are the recipients
of every promise Jesus came to fulfill.
He bridged the gap between us and God's blessings—
and they are more than we can imagine.
When we seek Him,
our steps take us in the direction
of every good thing He has for us.

Let all who seek You rejoice and be glad in You;
let those who love Your salvation continually say,
"The LORD is great!"
PSALM 40:16

If we ask, then we will receive from God.
He says ask for wisdom, and He'll give it.
He gives the wisdom to walk in His footsteps each day,
and be a light to others wherever we go.

I pray that the God of our Lord Jesus Christ,
the glorious Father, would give you
the Spirit of wisdom and revelation in the knowledge of Him.
EPHESIANS 1:17

God meets all our needs each day.
And that fulfillment is a reflection of His love,
a revelation of His character,
and a reminder that we are His—
and each of us is priceless to Him.

Blessed is the God and Father of our Lord Jesus Christ,
who has blessed us with every spiritual blessing
in the heavens in Christ.
EPHESIANS 1:3

When the Holy Spirit has His way,
He will find comfort in our presence
and fill our surroundings with His presence.

When the Spirit of truth comes,
He will guide you into all the truth.
For He will not speak on His own,
but He will speak whatever He hears.
He will also declare to you what is to come.
JOHN 16:13

$\mathcal{W}$e can see with heaven's eyes
the fulfillment of our every need
as He blesses us with abundance.

*And my God will supply all your needs
according to His riches in glory in Christ Jesus.*
PHILIPPIANS 4:19

*G*od leads us to the places
where trust leaves no room for worry
and hope lifts us above every care.

*I will be the same until your old age,
and I will bear you up when you turn gray.
I have made you, and I will carry you;
I will bear and rescue you.*
ISAIAH 46:4

FEBRUARY 18

God loves perfectly;
God forgives completely;
God cares constantly.

May integrity and what is right watch over me,
for I wait for You.
PSALM 25:21

God's wisdom will always lead us to the right end
and bring us there in the best and highest way possible.
God knows exactly what He is doing with each of us.
He is the most qualified to run our lives.
He orders our steps, guides our way,
and handles our affairs.

The LORD will fulfill His purpose for me.
LORD, Your faithful love endures forever;
do not abandon the work of Your hands.
PSALM 138:8

God can easily rekindle the passion
in our dreams and fill us with the desire
to see them come true.

May Your faithful love rest on us, LORD,
for we put our hope in You.
PSALM 33:22

God honors our desire to follow Him
and guards our steps as we walk by faith.

*The desire of the righteous
turns out well.*
PROVERBS 11:23

The Lord blesses us with more hope
than our hearts can hold...
and uses the overflow to fill us
with the courage to do
what we thought impossible.

*He causes us to be devoted to Him, to walk in all His ways,
and to keep His commands, statutes, and ordinances,
which He commanded our ancestors.*
I KINGS 8:58

*Every need that ever existed
has an answer in Christ Jesus.*

*Holy, holy, holy, Lord God, the Almighty,
who was, who is, and who is to come.*
REVELATION 4:8

With God, our abilities skyrocket
as He fills our gaps and takes us in directions
we could never imagine without Him.

Jesus said to him,
"'If you can?' Everything is possible
for the one who believes."
MARK 9:23

*O*ur journey is showered
with the blessings of God,
and those blessings can become road signs
that lead to His best.

Nothing will be impossible with God.
LUKE 1:37

We can all experience the joy of His table—
the banquet He sets for us—
in the presence of our enemies.
His joy is our strength!

Because of my adversaries,
show me Your way, LORD,
and lead me on a level path.
PSALM 27:11

God is almighty. His power is limitless.
He never gets fatigued or worn down.
He will never face a situation He can't handle.
His eternal power allows Him to say,
"There is nothing too hard for Me."

I am at rest in God alone;
my salvation comes from Him.
He alone is my rock and my salvation, my stronghold;
I will never be shaken.
PSALM 62:1-2

God has prepared this day perfectly,
and put His blessing upon it—
just because He loves us.

Help me stay on the path of Your commands,
for I take pleasure in it.
PSALM 119:35

God designs every day with His children in mind.
There is nothing He hasn't thought of
and planned for where we are concerned.

This is the day the LORD has made;
let us rejoice and be glad in it.
PSALM 118:24

God blesses His children with courage
to do the extraordinary.
He created us with that in mind.

I have loved you with an everlasting love;
therefore, I have continued to extend faithful love to you.
JEREMIAH 31:3

The simple, sure, constant truth of God's breath
in our lungs is a gift He gives
to remind us of His constant provision.
He gives to us again and again,
as often as we need.

Our Lord and God, You are worthy
to receive glory and honor and power,
because You have created all things,
and by Your will they exist and were created.
REVELATION 4:11

MARCH 4

*D*eep in each child of God's heart
is the knowledge of just how loved we are
by our Father in heaven.

I will praise You because I have been
remarkably and wondrously made.
Your works are wondrous, and I know this very well.
PSALM 139:14

*E*ach day begins and ends
with the chance to sense
the Lord's peaceful presence...
a quietness of heart...
and a thankfulness of spirit.

What no eye has seen, no ear has heard,
and no human heart has conceived—
God has prepared these things
for those who love Him.
I CORINTHIANS 2:9

MARCH 6

*W*alking with God is full of scenic views,
rich valleys, arid deserts,
and amazing pathways.
It's all valuable as long as
we walk together with Him.

You reveal the path of life to me;
in Your presence is abundant joy;
at Your right hand are eternal pleasures.
PSALM 16:11

*A*s we walk with God,
we don't need to worry about how tight
the grip of our hand is upon His...
He is the one who is holding on to us!

For I am the LORD your God,
who holds your right hand, who says to you,
"Do not fear, I will help you."
ISAIAH 41:13

The Lord abundantly blesses our hopes and dreams,
brings blessings out of our trials and challenges,
and blesses others through our hands and hearts.

Let your graciousness be known to everyone.
The Lord is near. Don't worry about anything, but in everything,
through prayer and petition with thanksgiving,
present your requests to God.
PHILIPPIANS 4:5, 6

*W*hen we trust God,
His hands can be our hands,
His feet can be our feet,
and His heart can be our heart.

*In the same way,
let your light shine before others,
so that they may see your good works and
give glory to your Father in heaven.*
MATTHEW 5:16

MARCH 10

Each day is filled with ways
to appreciate our ability to serve God
and walk in thankfulness
for all He has done for others through us.

God is not unjust;
He will not forget your work
and the love you demonstrated
for His name by serving the saints.
HEBREWS 6:10

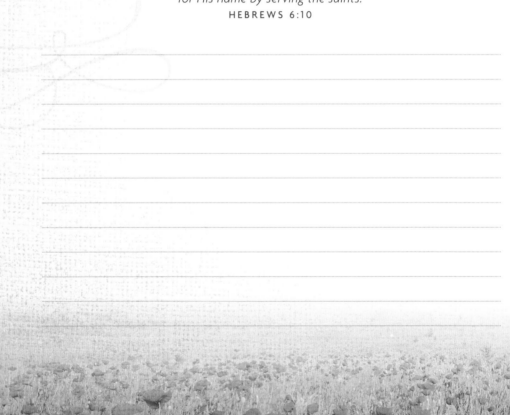

*W*hen we begin our praise,
we find His face.
Then awe will turn our praise
into a true response of worship.

Worship the Lord your God,
and serve only Him.
MATTHEW 4:10

MARCH 12

The Lord gives grace to see how truly blessed we are,
how truly surrounded by His love are our lives.
He then gives us great joy in spilling out that love
and blessing to everyone around us.

I will bless you...
and you will be a blessing.
GENESIS 12:2

*E*ach day is full of hope and purpose.
It's up to us to grab hold of those reigns
and start riding!

And whatever you do, in word or in deed,
do everything in the name of the Lord Jesus,
giving thanks to God the Father through Him.
COLOSSIANS 3:17

God watches over our coming and going.
He will never steer us wrong.
He will always be there,
even when we don't feel Him or hear a clear voice.
He will never leave us nor forsake us.

"For I know the plans I have for you"—
this is the LORD's declaration—
"plans for your well-being, not for disaster,
to give you a future and a hope."
JEREMIAH 29:11

There will never be a moment
in our days or a time in our lives
when God is not good to us.

Give thanks to the LORD, for He is good;
His faithful love endures forever.
PSALM 118:1

MARCH 16

*G*od blesses us each day—
blesses in a way that fills our hearts
with a thousand "thank you's"
for all that His hand brings our way.

The counsel of the LORD stands forever,
the plans of His heart from generation to generation.
PSALM 33:11

There is blessing in following our hearts—
God works out His will for our lives
through the desires He puts there.

Trust in the LORD with all your heart,
and do not rely on your own understanding;
in all your ways know Him,
and He will make your paths straight.
PROVERBS 3:5-6

_____
_____
_____
_____
_____
_____
_____
_____
_____
_____
_____

MARCH 18

*W*e can grow in intimacy
with the Lord every day—
getting to know His character and faithfulness
in the ways we most need
to experience Him.

I will bless the LORD who counsels me—
even at night when my thoughts trouble me.
PSALM 16:7

Today is ours to give back to God.
We can surrender our time, energy, focus,
and the work of our hands.
We can allow Him to use us how He will,
for His will—as He will.

*But seek first the kingdom of God and His righteousness,
and all these things will be provided for you.*
MATTHEW 6:33

*W*e are blessed by the Lord moment by moment;
for with every breath we have an opportunity
to praise Him, serve Him, love Him.

May the words of my mouth
and the meditation of my heart
be acceptable to You, LORD,
my rock and my Redeemer.
PSALM 19:14

*W*hen we ask,
God allows us to see His gifts surrounding us,
opening all of our senses to His beauty.

Let everything that breathes praise the LORD.
PSALM 150:6

*G*od's desire to bless us
is as great as He is...
and impossible to fathom.

The LORD's blessing enriches,
and He adds no painful effort to it.
PROVERBS 10:22

Even when God says no
to something in our lives,
He is saying yes
to something better.

For every one of God's promises is "Yes" in Him.
Therefore, through Him
we also say "Amen" to the glory of God.
II CORINTHIANS 1:20

MARCH 24

*N*o matter what we face each day...
a little thing or a huge one,
a cascade of things
or just a simple ordinary day...
He's got us covered.

For as high as the heavens are above the earth,
so great is His faithful love toward those who fear Him.
PSALM 103:11

*W*e have a special place in God's plan—
and our steps are ordered by Him
and blessed with peace
when we choose to follow His lead.

The one who understands a matter finds success,
and the one who trusts in the LORD
will be happy.
PROVERBS 16:20

The work before us is there for us to enjoy—
and we bless His heart when we approach it
as if God is the only One we're working for.

The LORD your God blesses you
as He has promised you.
DEUTERONOMY 15:6

Sometimes it takes courage to give thanks
in all things and strength
to give thanks for all things.
But we can always give thanks to the Lord,
for He is good.

Let us continually offer up to God a sacrifice of praise,
that is, the fruit of lips that confess His name.
HEBREWS 13:15

*W*hen we follow God,
it delights Him to bless us
with a will to work for Him,
favor to follow Him,
and anointing to amaze those around us
with His incredible love.

*Whatever you do, do it from the heart,
as something done for the Lord and not for people,
knowing that you will receive the reward
of an inheritance from the Lord.
You serve the Lord Christ.*
COLOSSIANS 3:23, 24

*W*e can live with enthusiasm
for the purpose we were created to fulfill—
and a fresh sense of knowing how important it is.

*Give...and the LORD your God will bless you
in all your work and in everything you do.*
DEUTERONOMY 15:10

Following the Lord
is rarely a straight path...
but it is always an amazing adventure.

Many plans are in a person's heart,
but the LORD's decree will prevail.
PROVERBS 19:21

Every time we give thanks with our voices,
we are saying with our hearts
that God is taking good care of us.

Give thanks in everything;
for this is God's will for you in Christ Jesus.
I THESSALONIANS 5:18

*I*f we let them,
our trials lead us to a closer relationship with God,
and become a threshold for even greater blessings
in our lives.

Rejoice in all the good things
the LORD your God has given you
and your household.
DEUTERONOMY 26:11

God blesses us with every fruit of the Spirit...
including patience as we wait on Him each day.

Blessed is the one who endures trials,
because when he has stood the test
he will receive the crown of life
that God has promised to those who love Him.
JAMES 1:12

God is the best source of unwavering confidence
that we can do anything He calls us to do.
He is the best assurance that when we do
what He calls us to, it will be blessed.

There is no distinction between Jew and Greek,
because the same Lord of all richly blesses all who call on Him.
ROMANS 10:12

*W*hen in doubt, shout!
We may not be able to change our circumstances,
but praise is the fastest way
to turn our own attitudes around.

For the vision is yet for the appointed time;
it testifies about the end and will not lie.
Though it delays, wait for it,
since it will certainly come and not be late.
HABAKKUK 2:3

*L*iving in the aim of His presence
and purpose is success
in the kingdom of God.

Vindicate me, LORD,
because I have lived with integrity
and have trusted in the LORD without wavering.
PSALM 26:1

*W*isdom is a blessing—we can walk in it;
joy is a gift—we can be generous with it;
prayer is a privilege—we can act on it;
love is a miracle—we can be God's messengers.

*For the LORD will be your confidence
and will keep your foot from a snare.*
PROVERBS 3:26

The Lord knows exactly what today holds.
And we know Who holds
this day in the palm of His hand...
so all we need to do is ask Him to lead on.

Teach us to number our days carefully
so that we may develop wisdom in our hearts.
PSALM 90:12

*H*aving a good day doesn't mean having an easy
or perfect day. It means a day spent
saying "yes" to God's purpose.
A day lived in the will of God is the best day
anyone could ever spend.

*That you may be filled with the knowledge
of His will in all wisdom and spiritual understanding.*
COLOSSIANS 1:9

*W*e can always go about our day
with a quiet heart,
knowing that God is taking care of everything
that concerns us.

For in Christ Jesus neither circumcision
nor uncircumcision accomplishes anything;
what matters is faith working through love.
GALATIANS 5:6

*W*e are most at peace
when we recognize our heavenly place,
high above the trauma and drama
of this world.

A tranquil heart is life to the body,
but jealousy is rottenness to the bones.
PROVERBS 14:30

Joy comes from a deep-seated trust
that God is in control
of everything that concerns us—
and we can walk through each day
knowing every need we have is met in full.

The LORD will always lead you,
satisfy you in a parched land, and strengthen your bones.
You will be like a watered garden
and like a spring whose water never runs dry.
ISAIAH 58:11

The Father's kindness is a salve to the heart.
He is constantly choosing to demonstrate
His love through being kind to us.

*May the LORD show kindness
and faithfulness to you.*
II SAMUEL 2:6

If we ask, God will show us
just what we mean to Him.
Our value is priceless in His eyes,
and He delights to show us in the ways
we most need to experience it.

Consider the birds of the sky:
They don't sow or reap or gather into barns,
yet your heavenly Father feeds them.
Aren't you worth more than they?
MATTHEW 6:26

God blesses us with wisdom in our decisions—
Strength in our responsibilities—
Success in our endeavors—
Joy in our commitments—
Peace in our relationships—
Love in everything!

LORD, I am indeed your servant...
You have loosened my bonds.
PSALM 116:16

*W*isdom is readily available,
because God is not a stingy giver.
He pours out wisdom as we ask.

Who among you is wise and understanding?
By his good conduct he should show that his works
are done in the gentleness that comes from wisdom.
JAMES 3:13

*H*is presence is always near
and His peace is always available.
We can always just be still,
and consciously know that
God is in our midst.

*He has saved us and called us
with a holy calling, not according to our works,
but according to His own purpose and grace,
which was given to us in Christ Jesus before time began.*
II TIMOTHY 1:9

APRIL 17

Our hearts are made to always know the Lord...
Our feet are made to always follow His path...
Our lives are made to always be blessed by Him!

Now if any of you lacks wisdom, he should ask God—
who gives to all generously and ungrudgingly—
and it will be given to him.
JAMES 1:5

*W*e can trust that the God of every blessing,
who is good in every way,
will rest His hand upon us
and bring joy.

God, create a clean heart for me
and renew a steadfast spirit within me.
PSALM 51:10

*G*od is a giver
of every good and perfect gift,
and we are daily recipients
of all He has to offer.

You open Your hand and satisfy
the desire of every living thing.
PSALM 145:16

The freedom that the Lord gives us as His servants is that everything we do is for His approval and not for the recognition of others.

For you were called to be free, brothers and sisters;
only don't use this freedom as an opportunity for the flesh,
but serve one another through love.
GALATIANS 5:13

The blessings of the Lord
are always available to us...
They rest upon us, dwell within us,
and flow through us.

You have encircled me;
You have placed Your hand on me.
PSALM 139:5

The Lord never leaves us stagnant.
Even when we feel alone or lost...
we can simply believe in Him
and He will lift us up in due time.

*The one who believes in Me,
as the Scripture has said,
will have streams of living water
flow from deep within him.*
JOHN 7:38

*G*od loves each of us so dearly.
He delights to speak blessings
and comfort to our hearts
when we need it most.

If you remain in Me and My words remain in you,
ask whatever you want and it will be done for you.
My Father is glorified by this: that you produce much fruit
and prove to be My disciples.
JOHN 15:7-8

*H*oly Spirit is the most incredible gift.
He is constantly comforting, guiding, and helping.
When we allow Him to work in us,
there is no end to the depth of peace we will know.

We know that all things work together
for the good of those who love God,
who are called according to His purpose.
ROMANS 8:28

God can fill us
with the confident knowledge
of His protection as He fights our battles.
All we need to do is ask.

My shield is with God,
who saves the upright in heart.
PSALM 7:10

Today and always,
we can experience God's love and joy...
and our lives can be filled with the blessings of
His goodness and grace.

Test me, LORD, and try me;
examine my heart and mind.
For Your faithful love guides me,
and I live by Your truth.
PSALM 26:2-3

APRIL 27

God's grace is enough for every situation.
In our weakness He is strong,
and we can always ask for the evidence
of that knowledge in our lives.

*Indeed, we have all received grace upon grace
from His fullness.*
JOHN 1:16

$\mathscr{L}$ife's an adventure.
We don't know how God will direct us
from where we stand now.
We need to trust Him to show us the way,
and He will reveal it in love.

Rejoice in hope; be patient in affliction;
be persistent in prayer.
ROMANS 12:12

*G*od has blessed each of us with
the ability to achieve our goals...
the courage to pursue our dreams...
the faith to believe in His promises.

*And God is able to make every grace overflow to you,
so that in every way, always having everything you need,
you may excel in every good work.*
II CORINTHIANS 9:8

The victory of Jesus is always available
to strengthen our hearts and quicken our steps,
today and every day.

Keeping our eyes on Jesus,
the source and perfecter of our faith.
For the joy that lay before Him,
He endured the cross, despising the shame,
and sat down at the right hand of the throne of God.
HEBREWS 12:2

*T*he Lord's thoughts and His heart
are toward His children—
to keep us, to guide us,
and to bless us as only He can.

Be strong and courageous;
don't be terrified or afraid of them.
For the LORD your God is the One who will go with you;
He will not leave you or abandon you.
DEUTERONOMY 31:6

*O*ur lives may be busy at times and quiet at times,
but when God orders our steps
and puts His purposes in our hearts,
our lives will never be meaningless.

Do not lack diligence in zeal;
be fervent in the Spirit;
serve the Lord.
ROMANS 12:11

*God's love allows the roots of our faith
to grow deep as we learn to trust Him.*

*The LORD will protect you from all harm;
He will protect your life.*
PSALM 121:7

God chooses us and draws us to His side—
He calls us and equips us for His work—
He blesses us and gifts us to fulfill His purposes.

Happy are those who keep His decrees
and seek Him with all their heart.
PSALM 119:2

The Lord loves to reward
His faithful children.

Great and mighty God whose name is the LORD of Armies,
the One great in counsel and powerful in action.
Your eyes are on all the ways of the children of men
in order to reward each person according to his ways
and as the result of his actions.
JEREMIAH 32:18, 19

The good, the bad, and the ugly—
nothing surprises or perplexes God.
He only lets what He can use take place.

Acknowledge that the LORD is God.
He made us, and we are His—
His people, the sheep of His pasture.
PSALM 100:3

The Lord enjoys blessing us
with all the things that will assure us of His love,
His presence, and His daily care for us.

I call to God Most High,
to God who fulfills His purpose for me.
PSALM 57:2

Each day is a grand opportunity
to pour ourselves out in love
and receive His overflowing love in return.

Little children, let us not love in word or speech,
but in action and in truth.
This is how we will know that we belong to the truth
and will reassure our hearts before Him.
I JOHN 3:18-19

MAY 9

*T*oday has been designed to remind us
that God has given us a fresh start, a new hope,
and hearts filled with reasons to be thankful.

Because of the LORD's faithful love we do not perish,
for His mercies never end.
LAMENTATIONS 3:22, 23

Apart from Jesus, life is empty.
But we are all things in Christ.

*Every good and perfect gift is from above,
coming down from the Father of lights,
who does not change like shifting shadows.*
JAMES 1:17

MAY 11

*T*oday we can be sure that in each of us,
God has created someone very special.

*Don't worry about anything, but in everything,
through prayer and petition with thanksgiving,
present your requests to God.*
PHILIPPIANS 4:6

*G*od is the perfect judge...
the source of love...
the reason we can live joyfully
through every situation.

Blessings are on the head of the righteous,
but the mouth of the wicked conceals violence.
PROVERBS 10:6

In all things, Jesus is
the strength of our hearts,
the center of our lives,
the guide of our futures,
the joy of our souls.

May the LORD bless you…
all the days of your life.
PSALM 128:5

The best place to be is under His care;
the safest place to be is in His will.

Be gracious to me, God, be gracious to me,
for I take refuge in You.
I will seek refuge in the shadow
of Your wings until danger passes.
PSALM 57:1

MAY 15

There is nothing God won't do
to pour out His love for us.
We love, because He loves us so much.

*Love the LORD your God
with all your heart,
with all your soul,
and with all your strength.*
DEUTERONOMY 6:5

God delights in giving us good health,
protecting us with His almighty strength,
and keeping us always in His tender care.

For He will give His angels orders concerning you,
to protect you in all your ways.
They will support you with their hands
so that you will not strike your foot against a stone.
PSALM 91:11-12

God can give miracles of strength and healing.
He gives His hand of restoration and refreshment.
He pours out His power in our lives
and the lives of those around us.
It's possible to come away from today
with a testimony of His great faithfulness!

I am the LORD who heals you.
EXODUS 15:26

It is such a gift to be comfortable in our own shoes,
walking in step with the Savior
and reveling in the uniqueness given us
by our Father in heaven.

*But the humble will inherit the land
and will enjoy abundant prosperity.*
PSALM 37:11

MAY 19

The Lord has a purpose
for each of us to fulfill...
power to equip us...
and strength to uphold us.

LORD, You do not withhold Your compassion from me.
Your constant love and truth will always guard me.
PSALM 40:11

There is never a reason to doubt God's power—
He is bigger than any problem
and more faithful than any man-made solution.

*Be strengthened by the Lord
and by His vast strength.*
EPHESIANS 6:10

When the Lord adds
His blessing to our lives,
there's no limit to our success!

The name of the LORD is a strong tower;
the righteous run to it and are protected.
PROVERBS 18:10

*E*very time we gaze at the stars in the sky,
we have the chance to see
the gleam of God's majesty and handiwork...
and opportunity to remain deeply in awe.

Let the whole earth fear the LORD;
let all the inhabitants of the world stand in awe of Him.
PSALM 33:8

*G*od promises to lead
and guide us no matter what.
We can listen, watch, pray,
and step forward in faith.

*Commit your activities to the LORD,
and your plans will be established.*
PROVERBS 16:3

*O*ur lives have the potential
to bring glory to the Father,
and blessing to us, in every way.

LORD, please grant us success!
He who comes in the name of the LORD is blessed.
PSALM 118:25, 26

MAY 25

*W*hen our hearts are bursting with praise,
and when thankfulness falls from our lips like rain,
the Lord is most blessed.

*My lips will glorify You
because Your faithful love is better than life.*
PSALM 63:3

The goodness of God brings joy.
His ways are right and lead to wisdom.
He is always true, always pure, and always sure—
bringing us freedom, refreshment, and strength.

I am the vine; you are the branches.
The one who remains in Me and I in him produces much fruit,
because you can do nothing without Me.
JOHN 15:5

This day has the potential
to reveal God's love for us...
and as we walk in the blessings He gives,
we can know the fullness of His joy.

But You, LORD, are a shield around me, my glory,
and the One who lifts up my head.
PSALM 3:3

*W*hen we ask,
we will receive His very best gifts.

And I pray this:
that your love will keep on growing in knowledge
and every kind of discernment,
so that you may approve the things that are superior
and may be pure and blameless in the day of Christ.
PHILIPPIANS 1:9-10

*L*ike the roots of a tree,
we can plant our trust deep in the Lord...
Like the branches of the tree,
we can reach out for new discoveries of His love...
Like the fruit of the tree,
we can continue to allow God
to make our life a blessing.

Walk in love, as Christ also loved us and gave Himself for us,
a sacrificial and fragrant offering to God.
EPHESIANS 5:2

We are loved and cared for
every moment by the God
who holds the universe
in His hands.

Sing to God! Sing praises to His name.
Exalt Him who rides on the clouds.
PSALM 68:4

As we abide in the Vine,
the Lord promises to grow and mature us.
All we need to do is stay close.

But the fruit of the Spirit is love, joy, peace,
patience, kindness, goodness, faithfulness,
gentleness, and self-control.
The law is not against such things.
GALATIANS 5:22, 23

*E*ach day is blessed
with little glimpses of God's love—
all we need to do is look around us.

The person who trusts in the LORD,
whose confidence indeed is the LORD, is blessed.
He will be like a tree planted by water:
it sends its roots out toward a stream,
it doesn't fear when heat comes,
and its foliage remains green.
JEREMIAH 17:7, 8

JUNE 2

If we open our eyes to the world around us,
He will surprise us with all the ways He shows
His love through nature, people,
and unexpected blessings.

For His invisible attributes, that is,
His eternal power and divine nature,
have been clearly seen since the creation of the world,
being understood through what He has made.
ROMANS 1:20

As we look to the future
and wonder what we'll go through,
we can be sure that the God of our yesterdays
is also the God of our todays and tomorrows.

I remember the days of old;
I meditate on all You have done;
I reflect on the work of Your hands.
PSALM 143:5

The blessings of the Lord
are constant reminders
of His hope...His joy...
His victory!

God's love was revealed among us in this way:
God sent His one and only Son into the world
so that we might live through Him.
I JOHN 4:9

Oh, what joy to be in His hands...
there is nothing that a person and the Lord
cannot do together.

You have given me the shield of Your salvation;
Your right hand upholds me,
and Your humility exalts me.
PSALM 18:35

JUNE 6

*G*od's purpose leads us through the day...
His counsel guides us in every situation...
His wonderful love blesses us wherever He leads.

He stores up success for the upright;
He is a shield for those who live with integrity.
PROVERBS 2:7

*E*very time we set our minds toward all
that God has done and all of who He is,
it's easy to be thankful.

Continue to live in Him,
being rooted and built up in Him and established in the faith,
just as you were taught, and overflowing with gratitude.
COLOSSIANS 2:6, 7

*G*od is always close
to our hearts and our circumstances.
He is always there to turn to
in love and trust.

For You are my rock and my fortress;
You lead and guide me for Your name's sake.
PSALM 31:3

How great God's love is for us!
How much He delights in us!
And how wonderful the blessings
of belonging to Him!

This God, our God forever and ever—
He will always lead us.
PSALM 48:14

*W*e belong to the Lord.
He made us. Chose us. Called us.
For those reasons alone,
we can keep making a difference wherever we are
and being who He created us to be.

I am the LORD.
I have called you for a righteous purpose,
and I will hold you by your hand.
I will watch over you.
ISAIAH 42:6

Victory is not found in the ease of our circumstances
nor in the strength of our own resources,
but in the presence of the Lord who is with us.

*Call to Me and I will answer you
and tell you great and incomprehensible things
you do not know.*
JEREMIAH 33:3

*W*e can know the fullness of God's joy in our days,
the closeness of His heart to our needs,
and the goodness of His plan for our lives.

The LORD values those who fear Him,
those who put their hope in His faithful love.
PSALM 147:11

*W*hen God calls someone,
no one else can take that place.
No one else can answer His call.
He'll be faithful to the one He called,
staying right there telling her
all she needs to know every day,
every step of the way.

For if you possess these qualities in increasing measure,
they will keep you from being useless or unfruitful
in the knowledge of our Lord Jesus Christ.
II PETER 1:8

Today is surrounded by God's love,
comforted by His grace,
blessed by His peace,
full of His presence,
and graced with His abundant joy.

My grace is sufficient for you,
for My power is perfected in weakness.
II CORINTHIANS 12:9

The heart is a fragile thing,
it can't be trusted to just anyone.
Thank goodness God isn't just anyone.

In all your ways know Him,
and He will make your paths straight.
PROVERBS 3:6

If only we could see the blessings
God has already prepared for us,
and He's preparing our hearts right now
to receive them.

I will send down showers in their season;
they will be showers of blessing.
EZEKIEL 34:26

*O*ur lives are made to always be abundant—
in joyful service, in daily blessings,
in abiding love.

*The LORD will open for you His abundant storehouse,
the sky, to give your land rain in its season
and to bless all the work of your hands.*
DEUTERONOMY 28:12

God loves the sound
of our voices in His ears...
and He loves when we listen to His.

But the righteous are glad;
they rejoice before God and celebrate with joy.
PSALM 68:3

*G*od hears our cries.
He knows the depths of our innermost being.
He is not indifferent to our cries for help.
He does not say to us,
"You should know better"
or "You don't need to be that way."
He comes to us in our need,
and He will never put us down.

*This poor man cried, and the LORD heard him
and saved him from all his troubles.*
PSALM 34:6

God's blessings are there for the receiving—
His abundant life...His pure love...
His perfect peace.

You will keep the mind
that is dependent on You in perfect peace,
for it is trusting in You.
ISAIAH 26:3

*G*od loves to give us fresh dreams,
new victories, and endless joys...
in surprising ways, unexpected blessings,
and overflowing measure!

*And the peace of God,
which surpasses all understanding,
will guard your hearts and minds in Christ Jesus.*
PHILIPPIANS 4:7

$\mathcal{W}$e can walk in His peace in quietness,
His beauty in stillness,
and sweet communion in His presence.

I will praise You, LORD, among the peoples;
I will sing praises to You among the nations.
PSALM 108:3

*W*ho would come for us
when we were so lost in our sin?
No one else but JESUS.
Who would seek us when we were
so far away from His heart?
No one else but JESUS.
Who would die for us
when we were so unresponsive to His love?
No one else but JESUS.

For You, LORD, bless the righteous one;
You surround him with favor like a shield.
PSALM 5:12

There isn't a moment of any day left to chance—
each one has been set into motion by God
for the blessing of our good and His glory.

But thanks be to God,
who gives us the victory
through our Lord Jesus Christ!
1 CORINTHIANS 15:57

God delights to overwhelm us with His goodness...
in the sweetest smell of a rose,
the gentleness of a hug,
or the bigness of His generosity toward us.

LORD, who is like You among the gods?
Who is like You, glorious in holiness,
revered with praises, performing wonders?
EXODUS 15:11

God can pour out confidence for His children
when we ask to understand our worth in His eyes—
we are His, we are valuable, we are blessed.

LORD, our Lord, how magnificent is
Your name throughout the earth!
You have covered the heavens with Your majesty.
PSALM 8:1

With such an enormous amount
of stuff to be learned, there are a million reasons
to thank God for being patient with us.

But You, Lord, are a compassionate and gracious God,
slow to anger and abounding in faithful love and truth.
PSALM 86:15

*T*oday is a day for happiness.
Today is a day where our faith can be
a source of strength, joy, and peace
to carry us through all our tomorrows.

*I am sure of this, that He who started a good work
in you will carry it on to completion
until the day of Christ Jesus.*
PHILIPPIANS 1:6

*W*e were each created in God's image—
and our actions are a reflection of His love.

May you be blessed by the LORD,
the Maker of heaven and earth.
PSALM 115:15

*W*e can let ourselves believe in great things—
God is in the habit of making them happen.

*You have put off the old self with its practices
and have put on the new self.
You are being renewed in knowledge
according to the image of your Creator.*
COLOSSIANS 3:9, 10

*E*ach of us has gifts
that are beyond compare...
and with God,
our dreams are always within reach.

My soul, bless the LORD,
and do not forget all His benefits.
PSALM 103:2

JULY 2

Today is a day for peaceful moments,
joyful memories, and beautiful miracles.

I will remember the LORD's works;
yes, I will remember Your ancient wonders.
PSALM 77:11

*W*e can expect our lives to be blessed—
it's impossible for God
to break His promises to us!

He remembers His covenant forever,
the promise He ordained
for a thousand generations.
PSALM 105:8

We can place our future into God's hands.
Our future is as bright as His promises!

You know with all your heart
and all your soul that none of the good promises
the LORD your God made to you has failed.
Everything was fulfilled for you; not one promise has failed.
JOSHUA 23:14

We can trust God when circumstances are
beyond our control.
We can trust Him in every interruption and delay.
We can trust Him through
every disappointment and heartache.
He is never surprised or caught off guard,
and He is concerned about
everything that concerns us.

Young lions lack food and go hungry,
but those who seek the LORD
will not lack any good thing.
PSALM 34:10

*L*ove is a choice, a commitment,
an action, a gift.
The spirit of God gives wisdom
to follow our hearts in the way of love.

Your kingdom is an everlasting kingdom;
Your rule is for all generations.
The LORD is faithful in all His words
and gracious in all His actions.
PSALM 145:13

$\mathcal{T}$here's no way to do life perfectly,
but there's a million ways
to do it with love.

Do everything in love.
I CORINTHIANS 16:14

JULY 8

*G*od would like to use today to teach us
more about His love for us
and His plan for our lives—
as long as our hearts are humble
and ready to learn.

*Neither death nor life, nor angels nor rulers,
nor things present nor things to come,
nor powers, nor height nor depth,
nor any other created thing
will be able to separate us from the love of God
that is in Christ Jesus our Lord.*
ROMANS 8:38-39

The Lord puts our feet on the path
He's chosen for us and
teaches our hearts to be content.

For the word of the LORD is right,
and all His work is trustworthy.
PSALM 33:4

*W*e can always remember
we are very special to God,
and He's always there to guide us, direct us,
and teach us as we seek to know His will.

Make Your ways known to me, LORD;
teach me Your paths.
PSALM 25:4

*L*ife is God's precious gift to us—
and it is our honor to spend it
bringing glory to Him.

Guide me in Your truth and teach me,
for You are the God of my salvation;
I wait for you all day long.
PSALM 25:5

Extravagant. Lavished. Forever.
Steadfast. Unending.
Perfect. Personal.
Just a few words to describe God's love for us!

I will praise You with all my heart, Lord my God,
and will honor Your name forever.
PSALM 86:12

The love of God is active goodness,
ceaseless mercy, and unending grace.
It wills the highest and chooses the best.
It encourages, supports, disciplines, edifies,
and corrects because it is holy love.

*Dear friends, let us love one another,
because love is from God,
and everyone who loves has been born of God
and knows God.*
I JOHN 4:7

JULY 14

The moment each of us was born,
God awakened the purpose He put within us—
and He is attentive to that purpose
every day of our lives.

*Proclaim the LORD's greatness with me;
let us exalt His name together.*
PSALM 34:3

$\mathcal{W}$e're never, ever alone.
Nothing takes God by surprise.
When we're weak, He's strong.
He's the God of new beginnings.
His love never gives up on us.

All the LORD's ways
show faithful love and truth.
PSALM 25:10

We can be strong in the Lord
and the power of His might today—
leaving every detail to Him.

Oh, Lord GOD!
You Yourself made the heavens and earth
by Your great power and with Your outstretched arm.
Nothing is too difficult for You!
JEREMIAH 32:17

$\mathcal{W}$e can let our days rest
in God's hands and
enjoy wherever life takes us.

A person's heart plans his way,
but the LORD determines his steps.
PROVERBS 16:9

God is always on our side,
even when things don't make sense.
He's for us when the road turns unexpectedly,
and He's ahead of us when we're not sure
how we're going to get through.

The LORD gives victory to His anointed;
He will answer him from His holy heaven
with mighty victories from His right hand.
PSALM 20:6

*W*e are priceless vessels of the love
God wants the world to see—
and He gives us opportunities
every day to express it.

I will most gladly boast
all the more about my weaknesses,
so that Christ's power may reside in me.
II CORINTHIANS 12:9

God is the strength, the hope,
and the One who will never fail us.
God is with us right now—
leading us in wisdom and love.

*May the Lord direct your hearts
to God's love and Christ's endurance.*
II THESSALONIANS 3:5

*W*e can trust Him daily.
We can trust Him moment by moment.
He is our life and our portion.
We can trust Him for everything and in everything.
He will never fail us nor let us down.

Trust in the LORD and do what is good;
dwell in the land and live securely.
PSALM 37:3

*W*e will be blessed when we hope.
We will be blessed when we trust.
We will be blessed when we cast all our cares on the Lord.

For God has not given us a spirit of fear,
but one of power, love, and sound judgment.
II TIMOTHY 1:7

The Lord's strong hand lifts our burdens
and refreshes our souls when we lean on Him.

Cast your burden on the LORD,
and He will sustain you;
He will never allow the righteous to be shaken.
PSALM 55:22

The work the Lord wants us
to do is revealed in the stillness
of trusting in Him.

*Those who know Your name trust in You
because You have not abandoned those
who seek You, LORD.*
PSALM 9:10

If we want to grow in beauty and in grace,
we simply need to ask God
which seeds to plant in the soil of our hearts.

Teach me, LORD, the meaning of Your statutes,
and I will always keep them.
Help me understand Your instruction,
and I will obey it and follow it with all my heart.
PSALM 119:33-34

In obedience, we can follow His footsteps...
In reflection, we can hear His voice...
In assurance, we can find His rest...
In labor, we can do His work...
In trust, we can find His strength.

You will be delivered by returning and resting;
your strength will lie in quiet confidence.
ISAIAH 30:15

*G*od is faithful,
and He knows the unspoken needs of our hearts.
We can rest in the assurance
that He'll meet them on time—
and generously.

Stop your fighting,
and know that I am God,
exalted among the nations,
exalted on the earth.
PSALM 46:10

*W*hen we are faithful, we are blessed.
God rewards us with countless loved ones
who choose to follow Christ
from one generation to another.

Know that the LORD your God is God,
the faithful God who keeps His gracious covenant loyalty
for a thousand generations with those
who love Him and keep His commands.
DEUTERONOMY 7:9

*T*here is no burden beyond His strength...
no boundaries to His love...
no limit to His mercies...
no problem outside His solution...
no need beyond His care.

I will bow down toward Your holy temple
and give thanks to Your name
for Your constant love and truth.
You have exalted Your name and
Your promise above everything else.
PSALM 138:2

Each person is a masterpiece of God—
filled with purpose...
eternally valued, infinitely loved.

We are His workmanship,
created in Christ Jesus for good works,
which God prepared ahead of time for us to do.
EPHESIANS 2:10

*G*od is there and He cares—
in goodness...in kindness...
in faithfulness...in love.

Your faithful love is as high as the heavens;
Your faithfulness reaches the clouds.
PSALM 57:10

AUGUST 1

The Lord is blessed when we reflect
the light of His love to those who cross our paths
because we can be confident
that He planned for our lives
to touch those around us.

The God of old is your dwelling place,
and underneath are the everlasting arms.
DEUTERONOMY 33:27

*L*ife in the Lord is
full of joy and generosity.

Bring joy to your servant's life....
You, Lord, are kind and ready to forgive,
abounding in faithful love to all who call on You.
PSALM 86:4, 5

*S*ometimes it's hard to see...
hard to believe...
but His light will always shine the way.

Happy are the people who know the joyful shout;
LORD, they walk in the light from Your face.
PSALM 89:15

*P*rayer is the powerful connection
between our needs and our God—
and He is always more than enough.

Consider me and answer, LORD my God.
Restore brightness to my eyes;
otherwise, I will sleep in death.
PSALM 13:3

We can experience the faithfulness of God
and the joys of following Him
in every single day and year ahead.

Happy is the one whose help is the God of Jacob,
whose hope is in the LORD his God.
PSALM 146:5

*G*od cares for us not because of what we do
but because of who we are.
We are His children and His responsibility.

Humble yourselves, therefore,
under the mighty hand of God...
casting all your cares on Him,
because He cares about you.
I PETER 5:6, 7

Our strength may fail, but our God will not—
the peace of heart and mind
that comes straight
from Him is available to us today.

The LORD will send His faithful love by day;
His song will be with me in the night—
a prayer to the God of my life.
PSALM 42:8

If we wait on God,
He will bring to pass all He has promised.
If we wait and rest in faith, then in His way,
He will provide at just the perfect time.

*God—He clothes me with strength
and makes my way perfect.*
PSALM 18:32

*T*oday we can trust God
to open our eyes and our hearts
to the needs of those around us—
and we can ask that more than anything else,
they see Him in us.

The LORD is my strength and my shield;
my heart trusts in Him, and I am helped.
Therefore my heart celebrates,
and I give thanks to Him with my song.
PSALM 28:7

If we open our hearts to God,
He will open the doors to our dreams.

The one who searches for
what is good seeks favor.
PROVERBS 11:27

God has brought us to this day,
and He will continue to lead and conform us
into His image and likeness.
In fact, we're looking more like Him every day!

We all, with unveiled faces,
are looking as in a mirror at the glory of the Lord
and are being transformed into the same image from glory to glory;
this is from the Lord who is the Spirit.
II CORINTHIANS 3:18

*W*e can be blessed in all we do,
confident that the spirit of God leads us
with wisdom and love.

Light dawns for the righteous,
gladness for the upright in heart.
PSALM 97:11

We can always find comfort
in God's unchanging promises
and His steadfast love.

*He leads the humble in what is right
and teaches them His way.*

PSALM 25:9

A heart that receives from God
has so many riches
to give to others.

*Only goodness and faithful love
will pursue me all the days of my life,
and I will dwell in the house of the LORD
as long as I live.*
PSALM 23:6

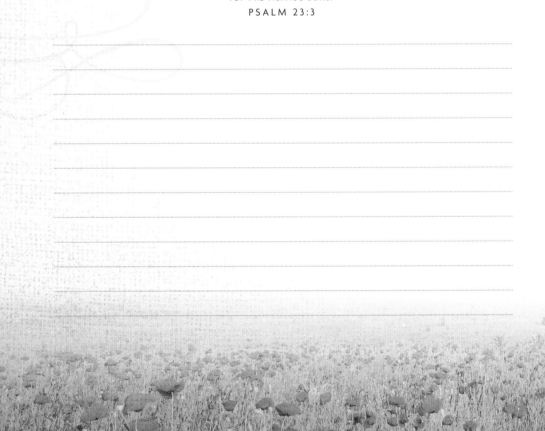

AUGUST 15

*T*oday we can experience a fresh sense
of God's presence in everything we do—
a sweet reminder that His mercies
are new every morning
and His love is boundless.

He renews my life;
He leads me along the right paths
for His name's sake.
PSALM 23:3

It is wonderful to wake up feeling
His presence and walk through the day
experiencing the many ways
He goes with us and works through us.

Do not fear, for I am with you.
ISAIAH 43:5

*W*e are blessed because we belong to God—
He chose us, shaped us,
and prepared us to make a difference
in the world.

I will be with you when you pass through the waters,
and when you pass through the rivers,
they will not overwhelm you.
ISAIAH 43:2

$\mathcal{L}$ife is all about loving God
and loving others—
it really is as simple as that.

We love because He first loved us.
The one who loves God
must also love his brother and sister.
I JOHN 4:19, 21

*G*od will not ask anything of us
that He hasn't empowered us
to accomplish or receive.
We simply need to believe.

Therefore, as God's chosen ones,
holy and dearly loved,
put on compassion, kindness, humility,
gentleness, and patience.
COLOSSIANS 3:12

AUGUST 20

It's so comforting to know that
the Lord never turns away from us.
In every moment, His hand is at work designing
what is best for our lives.

LORD, you are our Father;
we are the clay, and You are our potter;
we all are the work of Your hands.
ISAIAH 64:8

The Lord's thoughts
and His heart are toward us today—
to keep us, to guide us,
and to bless us as only He can.

Your eyes saw me when I was formless;
all my days were written in Your book
and planned before a single one of them began.
PSALM 139:16

There is never a time we're not in His heart,
never a time we're without love,
never a time when we're not blessed
with good things from above!

He did not even spare His own Son
but offered Him up for us all.
How will He not also with Him
grant us everything?
ROMANS 8:32

AUGUST 23

*T*he Lord helps us to rest in Him,
keep a quiet heart,
and look forward with hopeful expectation
to the things He is working together for good.

He will not allow your foot to slip;
your Protector will not slumber.
PSALM 121:3

God is here—to bring a ray of hope
that will light our tomorrow...
to carry us through in the arms of His grace...
to comfort our hearts
with His boundless love.

Rest in God alone, my soul,
for my hope comes from Him.
PSALM 62:5

*W*e can know the depth of God's desire to bless us—
His love is unconditional,
His promises are infallible,
and the good things He has planned for us
are unstoppable.

Please bless your servant's house
so that it will continue before You forever.
For You, Lord GOD, have spoken,
and with Your blessing Your servant's house
will be blessed forever.
II SAMUEL 7:29

Choosing happiness is always the best way.
We can find laughter and smiles around
every corner if we simply dare
to believe and look for them.

*Become mature, be encouraged,
be of the same mind, be at peace,
the God of love and peace will be with you.*
II CORINTHIANS 13:11

*E*very moment of the day,
God hears every heartbeat,
understands every thought,
and holds every person in the palm of His hand.

I will not forget you.
Look, I have inscribed you on the palms of My hands;
your walls are continually before Me.
ISAIAH 49:15, 16

As we face each new day, God wants to bless us.
He wants us to have joy, peace, hope,
and most of all, the inexpressible comfort of His love.

May Your faithful love comfort me.
PSALM 119:76

As our hearts worship Him,
we find the peace of God,
the joy of the Lord,
and the blessing of fellowship.

It is good to give thanks to the LORD,
to sing praise to Your name, Most High,
to declare Your faithful love in the morning
and Your faithfulness at night.

PSALM 92:1-2

God goes before us today,
and His presence is with us.
He has a life for us to live,
a plan for us to follow,
and a purpose for us to fulfill.

Remember what happened long ago, for I am God,
and there is no other; I am God, and no one is like Me.
I declare the end from the beginning,
and from long ago what is not yet done, saying:
My plan will take place, and I will do all My will.
ISAIAH 46:9-10

*G*od cannot break a single promise
He's made to anyone—
and every one of them
was written to bless His people.

God, who is rich in mercy,
because of His great love that He had for us,
made us alive with Christ even though we were dead in trespasses.
You are saved by grace!
EPHESIANS 2:4-5

In every promise that was fulfilled
through His birth, life, and resurrection,
we can find daily joy
and lasting peace in Jesus Christ.

*Let us hold on to the confession of our hope
without wavering,
since He who promised is faithful.*
HEBREWS 10:23

*W*e can live overjoyed to serve the Lord each day—
there's nothing more worthy of our time,
more nourishing to our souls,
or more satisfying to our spirits.

God—His way is perfect;
the word of the LORD is pure.
He is a shield to all who take refuge in Him.
II SAMUEL 22:31

The very best way to be enthusiastic
about life is to be truly passionate about God.

Happy is the person who fears the LORD,
taking great delight in His commands.
PSALM 112:1

We can take joy
in all we have in Jesus.
We can be sure that His constant love
will bless our days!

In the morning, LORD,
You hear my voice;
in the morning I plead my case to You
and watch expectantly.
PSALM 5:3

God's love is the most powerful,
life-changing force on earth—
and we can allow it to flow freely
through us each and every day.

What does the LORD your God ask of you
except to fear the LORD your God
by walking in all His ways, to love Him,
and to worship the LORD your God
with all your heart and all your soul?
DEUTERONOMY 10:12

God's continued blessings
bring beauty to our lives,
our relationships,
and our journeys with Him.

*This hope will not disappoint us,
because God's love has been poured out in our hearts
through the Holy Spirit who was given to us.*
ROMANS 5:5

The Lord is our faithful Shepherd;
our times are in His hands.
We can confidently step out
on the paths He's chosen for us.

The course of my life is in Your power.
PSALM 31:15

We are blessed
when we are in God's will—
His will is to heal us,
provide for us, protect us,
and daily give us the generous gifts of His grace.

His divine power has given us everything required for life
and godliness through the knowledge of Him
who called us by His own glory and goodness.
II PETER 1:3

*Prayer is powerful
because we believe in a God
who has all power.*

*This is the confidence we have before Him:
If we ask anything according to His will, He hears us.
And if we know that He hears whatever we ask,
we know that we have what we have asked of Him.*
1 JOHN 5:14-15

God calls each of us by name.
We are His beloved children,
the apple of His eye, and the delight of His heart.
Today we are in the exact place He wants us to be,
and tomorrow He will be
with us as He has always been—
in goodness, in kindness, and in faithfulness.

*The Lord is faithful; He will strengthen
and guard you from the evil one.*
II THESSALONIANS 3:3

Allow the blessings of the Lord
to settle gently in,
creating a beautiful place
for His joy to flourish.

You are my hiding place; You protect me from trouble.
You surround me with joyful shouts of deliverance.
PSALM 32:7

*W*e are blessed
when we allow the perfect peace
that only He can give to abide with us always
and in every way.

Peace I leave with you.
My peace I give to you.
I do not give to you as the world gives.
Don't let your heart be troubled or fearful.
JOHN 14:27

The sunrise ushers in
God's mercy toward us—
yesterday is forgotten,
today is in His hands,
and tomorrow is filled
with His promises.

*LORD, You will establish peace for us,
for You have also done all our work for us.*
ISAIAH 26:12

SEPTEMBER 14

*W*e can wait on God
to do His work in His perfect time and way,
and although the answer may seem slow,
He will not delay.

Wait for the LORD;
be strong, and let your heart be courageous.
Wait for the LORD.
PSALM 27:14

*D*eep down, our hearts know
what wise and wonderful creations we are—
beautifully designed, uniquely gifted,
lovingly expressed.

The LORD has promised good things.
NUMBERS 10:29

Isn't it amazing to know
the God of the universe set each of us apart
to be His very own?
We can let our hearts celebrate
being held in His hands,
loved by His heart,
and cradled in His care.

He will cover you with His feathers;
you will take refuge under His wings.
His faithfulness will be a protective shield.
PSALM 91:4

Jesus.
The Dayspring. Lamb of God.
Anointed One. Prince of Peace.
Savior. Righteous One. Lion of Judah.
Chief Shepherd. King of Israel.
Messiah.
We are blessed in many ways by Him
who is worthy of all our praise!

*Know that the LORD has set apart
the faithful for Himself;
the LORD will hear when I call to Him.*
PSALM 4:3

God's hand is extended to us—
not to push us away, but to draw us close;
not to keep us at a distance,
but to hold us near to His heart.

Display the wonders of Your faithful love,
Savior of all who seek refuge from those
who rebel against Your right hand.
PSALM 17:7

*I*t's never a question
of whether or not God will bless us—
it's a matter of having our faith
stretched out enough to receive
the incredible measure of goodness
God wants to pour into our lives!

*For He chose us in Him,
before the foundation of the world,
to be holy and blameless in love before Him.*
EPHESIANS 1:4

SEPTEMBER 20

*B*lue skies, the gentle breeze,
a single wildflower in a blanket of green...
God has set everything perfectly in place.

*In the beginning God created
the heavens and the earth.*
GENESIS 1:1

The Lord gives us strength when we're weary,
hope when we're disappointed,
and peace when we're anxious.

You will be enriched in every way for all generosity,
which produces thanksgiving to God through us.
II CORINTHIANS 9:11

All that God has done for us
is just the beginning of
all that He will do for us,
all that He will bring to us,
and all that He will be to us.

For everything was created by Him...
all things have been created through Him and for Him.
He is before all things,
and by Him all things hold together.
COLOSSIANS 1:16, 17

God has made each of us a gift to others.
We are seekers of truth and carriers of love.
And we are blessings to Him in ways
we don't yet understand!

Thanks be to God,
who always leads us in Christ's triumphal procession
and through us spreads the aroma
of the knowledge of Him in every place.
II CORINTHIANS 2:14

The Lord gives us
the incredible gifts of His grace—
all the things He gives out
of pure love, abundant mercy,
and sweet forgiveness.

*I am able to do all things
through Him who strengthens me.*
PHILIPPIANS 4:13

*W*hen a person chooses Jesus,
they can't help but be blessed.
That's part of the package!

*Since by the one man's trespass,
death reigned through that one man,
how much more will those who receive the overflow
of grace and the gift of righteousness reign
in life through the One man, Jesus Christ.*
ROMANS 5:17

We can confidently welcome the years
with arms open wide and love life
with the kind of passion
that comes straight from God.

*Indeed, if someone lives many years,
let him rejoice in them all.*
ECCLESIASTES 11:8

*E*ach day is a gift—
an opportunity to love God...
praise Him...
serve Him with all our hearts.

*For you are saved by grace through faith,
and this is not from yourselves;
it is God's gift.*
EPHESIANS 2:8

We are lights that can't help
but shine the moment
we open our eyes in the morning.
When God fills us with His light, we glow!

Let us not get tired of doing good,
for we will reap at the proper time
if we don't give up.
GALATIANS 6:9

The Lord gives priceless blessings—
the friendships He's created,
the family He's given,
the memories He's filled with His joy.

How happy are those who uphold justice,
who practice righteousness at all times.
Remember me, LORD,
when You show favor to Your people.
PSALM 106:3-4

*W*e can live life
with abundant love and laughter!
Every day is a celebration
of who we are in Christ.

*In Him we have also received an inheritance,
because we were predestined according
to the plan of the One who works out everything
in agreement with the purpose of His will.*
EPHESIANS 1:11

Today we can walk in His favor,
feeling His loving and guiding presence
every step of the way.

I will instruct you and show you the way to go;
with My eye on you, I will give counsel.
PSALM 32:8

The Lord is everything we need at all times—
we can count on Him to guard our steps,
bless the paths ahead of us,
and carry us when our strength is gone.

How happy is everyone
who fears the LORD, who walks in His ways!
You will surely eat what your hands have worked for.
You will be happy, and it will go well for you.
PSALM 128:1-2

The grace of God is lifting us from below,
carrying us through each moment and circumstance,
and sustaining us until our heads hit the pillow.

Those who trust in the LORD will renew their strength;
they will soar on wings like eagles;
they will run and not become weary,
they will walk and not faint.
ISAIAH 40:31

OCTOBER 4

It's such a joy to be the kind of person
who looks at a cloud and says,
"There's a rainbow coming in just a little while."
Then kicks off their shoes and dances in the puddles
until the sun comes out again.

Look, the LORD keeps His eye on those who fear Him—
those who depend on His faithful love.
PSALM 33:18

The Lord allows us to be His vessels—
He makes us keenly aware of His desire
to bless those around us.
He gives us the words to speak,
shows us the favor to extend,
and fills us with joy to share.

Save Your people, bless Your possession,
shepherd them, and carry them forever.
PSALM 28:9

The Lord searches our hearts
so that we may speak graciously.
He opens our ears at all times to hear truth
and pick up on others' needs
and opens our mouths only
when it's wise to speak.

Let your speech always be gracious, seasoned with salt,
so that you may know how you should answer each person.
COLOSSIANS 4:6

If we just look around us,
we can be reminded of the ways
God has met our needs in the past—
reassuring our hearts
of His constant love and faithfulness.

Blessed are the merciful,
for they will be shown mercy.
MATTHEW 5:7

*W*hen we confidently look toward the heavens,
we will know deep in our hearts
that everything is going to be more than OK—
it will work out perfectly.

Let us draw near with a true heart
in full assurance of faith.
HEBREWS 10:22

One of the greatest gifts
a person can give herself is
the ability to encourage herself
in seeking Him.

*You will seek Me and find Me
when you search for Me with all your heart.*
JEREMIAH 29:13

The Lord blesses our lives and shows us
how to be a blessing to others.
Our hearts can be a continual harvest of kindness,
generosity, joy, and love because of His grace.

*Therefore, I remind you
to rekindle the gift of God that is in you.*
II TIMOTHY 1:6

One of our greatest joys
lies in the discovery of
the hope of Jesus and the truth of His Word.
One of our greatest blessings is
in having more than enough
to pour out to those around us.

*Blessed are those
who hunger and thirst for righteousness,
for they will be filled.*
MATTHEW 5:6

*W*hen we sit quietly...
breathe deeply...hope steadily...
we will have the assurance
that God is working
on our behalf this very moment.

My faithful God will come to meet me;
God will let me look down on my adversaries.
PSALM 59:10

The Lord rewards us
with the gift of His love
and the simplicity of His grace;
He lets us discover His will for our lives
with patience and understanding;
He is a compassionate Father
and constant friend.

You show that you are Christ's letter,
delivered by us, not written with ink
but with the Spirit of the living God—
not on tablets of stone but on tablets of human hearts.
II CORINTHIANS 3:3

*W*e are tapped in to the Source of all sources,
and He promises to pour out wisdom
on those who ask.
So we need not be shy
before our Father in heaven—
if we ask, we will receive!

Our Lord is great, vast in power;
His understanding is infinite.
PSALM 147:5

The Lord listens closely to our prayers,
sees what our hearts need most,
and blesses our lives with His goodness.

*See what great love the Father has given us
that we should be called God's children—
and we are!*
1 JOHN 3:1

*G*od says anything is possible.
So we can live our lives believing it
with all of our hearts.

*My mouth will tell about Your righteousness
and Your salvation all day long,
though I cannot sum them up.
I come because of the mighty acts of the Lord GOD;
I will proclaim Your righteousness, Yours alone.*
PSALM 71:15-16

*H*is promises always match His priorities.
And He will deliver all that we need,
as long as we keep our eyes focused on His face.

*Your Father knows the things
you need before you ask Him.*
MATTHEW 6:8

The spirit of God delights
in showing us how precious we are to Him—
and how carefully and wonderfully
we were made for a special purpose.

You are precious in My sight and honored,
and I love you.
ISAIAH 43:4

*E*ach of us is, in God's eyes,

the cream of the crop.

He makes no mistakes,

so He made none in us.

We are all amazing and wonderful works!

For it was You who created my inward parts;
You knit me together in my mother's womb.
PSALM 139:13

God cares about everything
in our lives because
He cares so much about us.

*Those who put their hope in the LORD
will inherit the land.*
PSALM 37:9

We can be blessed today, and rejoice...
Jesus is praying for us!

*Christ Jesus is the One who died,
but even more, has been raised;
He also is at the right hand of God
and intercedes for us.*
ROMANS 8:34

Jesus lives!
And even right now,
He is at work to save, free,
and transform those
who come to God through Him.
Victory in Jesus!

Therefore, He is able to save completely
those who come to God through Him,
since He always lives to intercede for them.
HEBREWS 7:25

*W*hen God gives a gift,
it's eternally good—
and love is always
the reason He gives.

*When the kindness of God our Savior
and His love for mankind appeared, He saved us—
not by works of righteousness that we had done,
but according to His mercy.*
TITUS 3:4, 5

It's so easy to take a moment
to think about something wonderful God has done.
And that simple act can transform
attitudes in a moment!

Rejoice in the LORD, you righteous ones;
praise from the upright is beautiful.
PSALM 33:1

*W*e are truly alive today—
as free as butterflies
released from their cocoons.

Therefore, if anyone is in Christ,
he is a new creation;
the old has passed away,
and see, the new has come!
Everything is from God.
II CORINTHIANS 5:17, 18

God's peace is there to cover us,
His hope to inspire us,
His joy to uplift us,
and His love to surround us.

As for me, LORD,
my prayer to You is for a time of favor.
In Your abundant, faithful love, God,
answer me with Your sure salvation.
PSALM 69:13

Praise and thanks
will always open doors
to a better mood and a more accurate
view of the circumstances.

Enter His gates with thanksgiving
and His courts with praise.
Give thanks to Him and bless His name.
PSALM 100:4

$\mathcal{W}$e shouldn't hold back
a kind word or a loving deed—
they have God's blessing
all over them!

*The LORD watches over
the blameless all their days,
and their inheritance will last forever.*
PSALM 37:18

*G*lory to God for the gift of Jesus...
Praise to God for the joy of serving Him...
Thanks to God for the hope of seeing Him.

Dear friends, we are God's children now,
and what we will be has not yet been revealed.
We know that when He appears,
we will be like Him
because we will see Him as He is.
I JOHN 3:2

OCTOBER 30

If we were only aware of
how often He steps in for us!
Like a parent protecting a new toddler,
He follows, guides, and leads as we go.

Then we who are still alive, who are left,
will be caught up together with them
in the clouds to meet the Lord in the air,
and so we will always be with the Lord.
Therefore encourage one another with these words.
I THESSALONIANS 4:17-18

*W*ith God's help,
our words can be pleasing to Him,
our actions can honor Him,
and our lives can glorify Him.

*Blessed are the pure in heart,
for they will see God.*
MATTHEW 5:8

God has given us unique passion,
true determination, and powerful inner strength
to move forward in faith!

*One thing I do: Forgetting what is behind
and reaching forward to what is ahead.*
PHILIPPIANS 3:13

*W*hat Jesus did
paid the price for each one of us.
His actions provided us
with ALL FREEDOM in Him.

Now may the God of peace...
equip you with everything good to do His will,
working in us what is pleasing in His sight,
through Jesus Christ,
to whom be glory forever and ever.
HEBREWS 13:20, 21

*T*he blessing of prayer
is knowing God is listening...
and upholding every promise
He has made to us.

He has given us very great and precious promises.
II PETER 1:4

*G*od isn't some mean schoolmaster
waiting for us to guess the right answer.
He's there with His tender eyes on ours,
smiling, coaxing us toward truth.

He hears the prayer of the righteous.
PROVERBS 15:29

NOVEMBER 5

God paints every flower a beautiful hue...
and every life with a beautiful purpose.

He fulfills the desires of those who fear Him;
He hears their cry for help and saves them.
PSALM 145:19

Jesus—
His birth was a signal of hope...
His life a reflection of God...
His heart an expression of love.
We can experience the depth of that love
in every part of our day.

Glory to God in the highest heaven,
and peace on earth to people He favors!
LUKE 2:14

*H*is destiny was the cross…
His purpose was love…
His reason was us.
The blessings of our day can remind us
of all Jesus has given.

Thanks be to God for His indescribable gift!
II CORINTHIANS 9:15

People notice the surface things—
the cover of the book—
but God knows every single word
and letter and punctuation mark on the inside.
He has our stories memorized.

The gift of God is eternal life in Christ Jesus our Lord.
ROMANS 6:23

*W*hen the path ahead of us
is washed away,
God will give us wings.

I observed all the work of God and
concluded that a person is unable
to discover the work that is done under the sun.
Even though a person labors hard to explore it,
he cannot find it;
even if a wise person claims to know it,
he is unable to discover it.
ECCLESIASTES 8:17

All that is good is ours because of Jesus.
All that is fulfilling is ours because we serve Him.
All that is peaceful is ours because we love Him.

Do not be conformed to this age,
but be transformed by the renewing of your mind,
so that you may discern what is
the good, pleasing, and perfect will of God.
ROMANS 12:2

The Lord is with us through every circumstance—
the fun and the challenging.
He is in the business of working all things together
for His glory and invites us to share in His story.

You are to fear the LORD your God and worship Him. Remain faithful to Him and take oaths in His name.
DEUTERONOMY 10:20

The Lord often operates in abundance:
More joys than we expected...
bigger accomplishments than we dream of...
and greater gifts of His love than we can imagine!

Search me, God, and know my heart;
test me and know my concerns.
See if there is any offensive way in me;
lead me in the everlasting way.
PSALM 139:23-24

*G*od has given each of us
something we can give back to the world—
in a way no one else can.

He is always generous, always lending,
and his children are a blessing.
PSALM 37:26

A new day awaits us!
A new season in which we will
worry less and trust more.
A season with reduced fear
and enhanced faith.

You prepare a table before me
in the presence of my enemies;
You anoint my head with oil;
my cup overflows.
PSALM 23:5

NOVEMBER 15

*T*oday is one more chance
to laugh, listen, learn, and love.
And tomorrow, if it comes, we can do so again.

It is better to take refuge in the LORD
than to trust in humanity.
It is better to take refuge in the LORD
than to trust in nobles.
PSALM 118:8–9

The Lord has the means to help us remember
that we can't change tomorrow until tomorrow.
He can remind us that today, our job is to live today.
To face today's challenges with today's strength.
To dance today's waltz with today's music.
To celebrate today's opportunities with today's hope.

Don't worry about tomorrow.
MATTHEW 6:34

Every elegant detail
of who we are was designed
for the purposes of God.

Offer yourselves to God,
and all the parts of yourselves
to God as weapons for righteousness.
ROMANS 6:13

*W*e can choose to meditate on good things.
We can let anxious, negative thoughts leave our minds.
We cannot control the circumstances,
but we can always control what we think of them.

Trust in the LORD forever,
because in the LORD,
the LORD Himself, is an everlasting rock!
ISAIAH 26:4

If life gives us lemons,
we can choose the grace and
presence of mind to make ourselves
some lemonade.

For from Him and through Him and to Him are all things.
To Him be the glory forever.
ROMANS 11:36

The Lord fills our hearts with gratitude,
so that we might remain focused on the present.

I will rejoice and boast about You;
I will sing about Your name, Most High.
PSALM 9:2

*W*hen we get a glimpse at the beauty around us,
it's hard to believe—
but we can be sure it's true—
that it's nothing compared to the beauty within us.

I will rejoice and be glad in Your faithful love.
PSALM 31:7

This is the day the Lord has made!
Today is wonderful,
His gifts are extravagant,
and His love is obvious.
We are blessed!

Who is a God like you,
forgiving iniquity and passing over rebellion…?
He does not hold on to His anger forever,
because He delights in faithful love.
MICAH 7:18

We each have a role to play.
No one else can fill the space in this world
that we were designed to fill.

I am not ashamed,
because I know whom I have believed and
am persuaded that He is able to guard
what has been entrusted to me until that day.
II TIMOTHY 1:12

*P*eace is His readily available promise.
When we are still and know it—
then we'll feel it.

Return to your rest, my soul,
for the LORD has been good to you.
PSALM 116:7

NOVEMBER 25

The Spirit of God can empower us
to face every challenge with style and grace.
All we need to do is trust Him.

*In all these things we are more than conquerors
through Him who loved us.*
ROMANS 8:37

Jesus defines beauty—
and the more we let Him transform us,
the more beautiful we become.

Be careful to do as the LORD your God has commanded you...
so that you may live, prosper, and
have a long life in the land you will possess.
DEUTERONOMY 5:32-33

We are in God's story.
His plot line, His characters, His happy ending.
Anything else goes against His perfect plan.

He has made everything appropriate in its time.
He has also put eternity in their hearts.
ECCLESIASTES 3:11

Just as we can't fill a cup that's already full,
God needs room in us to pour out His goodness.
So we need not worry about spending kindness,
joy, peace, or any other fruit on others or this world.
He'll fill us up again!

There will be a blessing,
if you obey the commands of the LORD your God.
DEUTERONOMY 11:27

*W*hen we put our hearts into everything,
we begin to see what God will do through us.

Serve with a good attitude,
as to the Lord and not to people.
EPHESIANS 6:7

This world is overflowing with barely-seen miracles—
an ant crawling, the heat warming,
the children playing together.
Noticing the world is noticing
God's handiwork and generosity.

I rejoice that I have complete confidence in you.
II CORINTHIANS 7:16

*O*bedience is a powerful weapon
against the enemy and a powerful tool
for the Kingdom of God.

*In Him we have boldness and
confident access through faith in Him.*
EPHESIANS 3:12

The only "can't" in our vocabulary
should be applied to Satan.
As in, "He can't win; we can't lose against him;
he can't separate us from the love of Jesus."

I am like a miraculous sign to many,
and You are my strong refuge.
My mouth is full of praise and honor to You all day long.
PSALM 71:7-8

DECEMBER 3

The words of Jesus never say,
"When you have a need, go to someone else."
In our need, Jesus always says,
"Come to Me."

Come to Me, all of you who are weary and burdened,
and I will give you rest.
MATTHEW 11:28

*W*e are blessed
when we recognize our individual gifts,
and we are blessed when we give away all
that will give Him room
to fill us back up to overflowing.

According to the grace given to us,
we have different gifts.
ROMANS 12:6

*Righteousness, peace,
and joy are ours in the Holy Spirit!
What incredible gifts!*

*Let them give thanks to the LORD
for His faithful love and His wondrous works for all humanity.
For He has satisfied the thirsty and
filled the hungry with good things.*
PSALM 107:8-9

$\mathcal{W}$e can always be extravagant in hope.
We can spend it all right now
because we won't need it in heaven
when we're face to face with Jesus.

*Watch the blameless and observe the upright,
for the person of peace will have a future.*
PSALM 37:37

DECEMBER 7

*J*esus changes sinners into saints,
rebels into servants, and slaves into free men.
He takes the indifferent and gives them motivation;
He takes the idle and gives them purpose;
He takes the listless and gives them zeal;
He takes the has-beens and gives them a future;
and He takes the downcast and gives them a song.

*Then the One seated on the throne said,
"Look, I am making everything new."*
REVELATION 21:5

DECEMBER 8

Joy isn't so much a choice
as it is a choice for us to receive it.
Joy always exists.
His joy is our strength—
should we choose to say "yes please!"
and start dancing.

I will hope continually and will praise You more and more.
PSALM 71:14

DECEMBER 9

*W*e are most blessed
when we are first in partnership with the Holy Spirit,
then in partnership with the body of Christ.
We are most effective when we choose Jesus,
then choose His love.

The LORD gives His people strength;
the LORD blesses His people with peace.
PSALM 29:11

*W*e can be "all in" today—
and we'll discover that God is there with us.
We can be fully present and
fully experience His presence.

The God of peace will soon crush Satan under your feet.
The grace of our Lord Jesus be with you.
ROMANS 16:20

*A*ll we need to start our day is a simple prayer,
"Lord, lead the way."
Then we can just step out the door
with hearts full of courage.

Let me experience Your faithful love in the morning,
for I trust in You. Reveal to me the way
I should go because I appeal to You.
PSALM 143:8

For the joy set before Him,
Jesus endured the cross.
Whatever we're facing today,
we can be sure that the joy
on the other side is worth it.

*Now in Christ Jesus, you who were far away
have been brought near by the blood of Christ.*
EPHESIANS 2:13

As we keep pressing toward Jesus,
we can be confident that where we are today
is not where we'll be tomorrow.

I am with you always, to the end of the age.
MATTHEW 28:20

*W*e never need to fear the future.
The Lord is already there preparing the way.

Now this is what the LORD says—
the One who created you...
"Do not fear, for I have redeemed you;
I have called you by your name; you are Mine."
ISAIAH 43:1

*W*e can do great things
if we focus on the great God who created us!

*The people who know their God
will be strong and take action.*
DANIEL 11:32

*Each day is full of His grace,
and each tomorrow is primed to receive
the grace we need for that moment.*

*Haven't I commanded you: be strong and courageous?
Do not be afraid or discouraged,
for the LORD your God is with you wherever you go.*
JOSHUA 1:9

The Lord can show us clear ways that our gifts
and personalities are just right for our surroundings.
We can ask and He will show us the direction
He is leading us to go as we follow Him.

LORD, You have searched me and known me.
PSALM 139:1

A stick in a bundle can't be broken,
and the closer we are to Jesus,
the stronger we become.

A cord of three strands is not easily broken.
ECCLESIASTES 4:12

*T*oday is a great day to put on some hiking shoes
and head in the direction of our dreams—
God has prepared the path ahead of us.

Now faith is the reality of what is hoped for,
the proof of what is not seen.
HEBREWS 11:1

It's never too late.
Whatever we plant today
will bring a harvest in the future.

If anyone builds on the foundation
with gold, silver, costly stones, wood, hay, or straw,
each one's work will become obvious.
For the day will disclose it, because it will be revealed by fire;
the fire will test the quality of each one's work.
I CORINTHIANS 3:12-13

DECEMBER 21

Every worry or fear, every anxiety or concern,
can be traded for His perfect peace.

You will keep the mind that is dependent
on You in perfect peace,
for it is trusting in You.
ISAIAH 26:3

*G*od gives the grace we need
to keep our eyes on Jesus
instead of on circumstances.
We will feel His presence as we go through
every valley and climb over every mountain.

God—His way is perfect; the word of the LORD is pure.
He is a shield to all who take refuge in Him.
PSALM 18:30

*T*rials build patience, make us strong,
and teach us that prayer and risk
often go hand in hand.

Let endurance have its full effect,
so that you may be mature and complete,
lacking nothing.
JAMES 1:4

*B*eing seated in heavenly places with God
means that whatever our circumstances,
they can't swallow us because we are above them.

Do not fear, for I am with you;
do not be afraid, for I am your God.
I will strengthen you; I will help you;
I will hold on to you with My righteous right hand.
ISAIAH 41:10

DECEMBER 25

The Lord delights to reveal His true personality—
His amazing, understanding, loving, powerful nature—
to us at just the right times.

As long as I am in the world,
I am the light of the world.
JOHN 9:5

It is a blessing to be faced with impossible things—
because it's in the impossible
that God can begin to work miracles.

You are the God who works wonders.
PSALM 77:14

In hard times, we can be sure of three things—
we are stronger than we ever imagined,
Jesus is closer than we ever realized,
and we are loved more than we ever knew.

Don't be afraid, you who are treasured by God.
Peace to you; be very strong!
DANIEL 10:19

*W*hatever we've got today,
we can hand it over to Him.
It's amazing what He can do with faith
the size of a mustard seed.

Dear friends, if our hearts don't condemn us,
we have confidence before God and
receive whatever we ask from Him
because we keep His commands
and do what is pleasing in His sight.
1 JOHN 3:21-22

DECEMBER 29

*N*othing is too much for God.
Therefore, nothing is too much for us in Christ.

When he calls out to Me, I will answer him;
I will be with him in trouble.
I will rescue him and give him honor.
PSALM 91:15

As we present our requests to God,
we may not see Him act right away.
But He always hears, and always acts,
and always works for our good.

Therefore, let us approach the throne of grace with boldness,
so that we may receive mercy and
find grace to help us in time of need.
HEBREWS 4:16

God used the infinite resources of His goodness
to create us and spared no expense in pouring out
His generous gifts of love, grace, and mercy.

Praise Him for His powerful acts;
praise Him for His abundant greatness.
PSALM 150:2